READING POWER

Westward Ho!

BUFFALO SOLDIERS

AND THE WESTERN FRONTIER

EMILY RAABE

The Rosen Publishing Group's
PowerKids Press™
New York

Published in 2003 by The Rosen Publishing Group, Inc.
29 East 21st Street, New York, NY 10010

First Edition

Book Design: Michael DeLisio

Photo Credits: Cover © Robert Holmes/Corbis; pp. 4–5 © Hulton/ Archive/Getty Images; pp. 7, 15, 16–17 © North Wind Picture Archives; pp. 8–9 © Denver Public Library, Western History Collection, Images X–31418, NS–734; pp. 10–11 © Brian A. Vihander/Corbis; pp. 12–13 © Underwood & Underwood/Corbis; pp. 14, 19 © Corbis; p. 21 © TimePix

Library of Congress Cataloging-in-Publication Data

Raabe, Emily.
Buffalo soldiers and the western frontier / Emily Raabe.
   p. cm. — (Westward ho!)
Summary: Details the role played by African American soldiers, whom Native Americans called Buffalo Soldiers, in the wars of the nineteenth century.
Includes bibliographical references and index.
ISBN 0-8239-6495-7 (lib. bdg.)
1. African Americans—West (U.S.)—History—19th century—Juvenile literature. 2. African American soldiers—West (U.S.)—History—19th century—Juvenile literature. 3. United States. Army—African American troops—History—19th century—Juvenile literature. 4. Frontier and pioneer life—West (U.S.)—Juvenile literature. 5. Indians of North America—Wars—1866-1895—Juvenile literature. 6. West (U.S.)—History—1860-1890—Juvenile literature. [1. African Americans—History—19th century. 2. African American soldiers—History—19th century. 3. United States. Army.—African American troops. 4. Frontier and pioneer life—West (U.S.) 5. Indians of North America—Wars—1866-1895. 6. West (U.S.)—History—1860-1890.] I. Title.
E185.925 .R22 2003
978'.00496073—dc21

                                    2002000505

Contents

The Buffalo Soldiers

Buffalo soldiers were African American soldiers in the United States Army. They served in the western part of the United States from 1867 to about 1896. Their orders were to fight against Native Americans. Native Americans named these men buffalo soldiers because they thought that the troops were brave and strong, like the buffalo.

Buffalo soldiers were separated from other soldiers in the army.

5

African American Soldiers in the Civil War

During the Civil War, many freed African American slaves joined the Union Army. However, these African American soldiers were not allowed to fight alongside white Union soldiers. After the Civil War ended, the U.S. government created several African American army groups. Two of these groups were the 9th and 10th Cavalries.

Now You Know

About 186,000 African American soldiers were in the Civil War. About 38,000 of them died.

Many buffalo soldiers
fought in the Civil War.

BUFFALO SOLDIERS IN THE WEST

In 1866, the 9th Cavalry was formed in New Orleans, Louisiana. The soldiers were sent to Texas to guard settlers. Many settlers in Texas were fighting Native Americans.

Buffalo soldiers often had to set up camps in the places where they worked.

Native Americans were angry because people were moving onto their land. The buffalo soldiers fought against Native Americans so that the settlers could feel safe.

NOW YOU KNOW

The men joined the 9th Cavalry for five years and were given a room, food, and 13 dollars a month.

The buffalo soldiers of the 9th Cavalry also guarded stagecoaches and the mail carriers who rode on horseback. Mail carriers and stagecoach riders were often attacked by robbers and Native Americans.

Early mail carriers put mail in special bags on the sides of their horses. It took them about three weeks to get their mail across the country.

The 10th Cavalry was formed in Fort Leavenworth, Kansas, in 1866. These soldiers guarded the mail and protected settlers, too. The 10th Cavalry also explored over 34,000 miles of new territory in the West.

The buffalo soldiers helped bring law and order to the western wilderness.

They found water holes for settlers to use during the long trips through the deserts of the Southwest. They also discovered new places where cattle could feed.

The 10th Cavalry built more than 300 miles of new roads and laid over 200 miles of telegraph lines. They built settlements in the wilderness that later became towns and cities.

Buffalo soldiers built the first roads on some of the roughest land in the United States.

Riding rough trails in the West was full of dangers. Soldiers who got hurt did not have doctors to help them. Doctors were often hundreds of miles away.

15

A Buffalo Soldier's Life

The life of a buffalo soldier was hard. The soldiers worked seven days a week, all year long. The Fourth of July and Christmas were the only two days of rest they were given.

Buffalo soldiers traveled through the western deserts for up to six months at a time. They often rode 1,000 miles, doing their job in a land with very little water. Battling strong winds and rainstorms made their work even harder.

The buffalo soldiers had a lower number of soldiers who ran away than any other cavalry group in the U.S. Army.

17

Some white army officers, such as George Armstrong Custer, refused to work with African American soldiers. Also, many white settlers did not like the buffalo soldiers because they had a different skin color. Fighting people's unfair feelings and ideas was not easy for the buffalo soldiers.

George Armstrong Custer was killed in a battle with Native Americans.

The brave African American soldiers of the 9th and 10th Cavalries proudly fought for the United States. The buffalo soldiers were given some of the hardest jobs in the army. The work of the buffalo soldiers helped open the West to American settlement.

Buffalo soldiers from the 9th and 10th Cavalries

Fourteen buffalo soldiers received the Medal of Honor, the highest award given to soldiers in battle.

Glossary

cavalry (**kav**-uhl-ree) a group of soldiers who were trained to fight on horseback

Civil War (**sihv**-uhl **wor**) the war fought from 1861 to 1865 between the southern and northern parts of the United States

settlement (**seht**-l-muhnt) a place where people come to live; the act of people moving to a place to live

settlers (**seht**-luhrz) people who come to stay in a new country or place

stagecoaches (**stayj**-koh-chez) wagons pulled by horses that carried passengers, mail, and packages

telegraph (**tehl**-uh-graf) a machine that is used to send messages over long distances through electric wires

Union Army (**yoo**-nyuhn **ahr**-mee) the army that fought for the northern part of the United States during the Civil War

wilderness (**wihl**-duhr-nihs) a place with few or no people living in it

Resources

Books

The Buffalo Soldiers
by Taressa Stovall
Chelsea House Publishers (1997)

The Buffalo Soldiers
by Catherine Reef
Twenty-First Century Books (1993)

Web Sites

Due to the changing nature of Internet links, PowerKids Press has developed an online list of Web sites related to the subjects of this book. This site is updated regularly. Please use this link to access the list:

http://www.powerkidslinks.com/wh/buff/

Index

C
cavalry, 6, 8–10, 12, 14, 17, 20–21
Civil War, 6–7
Custer, George Armstrong, 18–19

D
deserts, 13, 17

N
Native Americans, 4, 8–10, 19

S
settlement, 14, 20
settlers, 8–9, 12–13, 18
stagecoaches, 10

T
territory, 12

U
Union Army, 6

W
West, 12, 15, 20

Word Count: 479

Note to Librarians, Teachers, and Parents

If reading is a challenge, Reading Power is a solution! Reading Power is perfect for readers who want high-interest subject matter at an accessible reading level. These fact-filled, photo-illustrated books are designed for readers who want straightforward vocabulary, engaging topics, and a manageable reading experience. With clear picture/text correspondence, leveled Reading Power books put the reader in charge. Now readers have the power to get the information they want and the skills they need in a user-friendly format.